NATHANIEL WILSON

$ave It!

Simple Ideas For Anyone To Build Their Savings

First edition

This book was professionally typeset on Reedsy.
Find out more at reedsy.com

Contents

Who Am I And Why Should You Read This Book? 1

We Suck At Saving 3

Where You Save Your Money Matters. A Lot. 4

This All Sounds Great, But I Can't Afford To Save... 7

Verizon Is Ripping You Off 12

A Social Life Comes With A Price Tag 14

Being Thrifty Is Nifty 15

Streaming Services Wash Your Money Away 16

Giving Credit Cards Credit Where It's Due 18

Saving The Best For Last 22

Who Am I And Why Should You Read This Book?

Before we get started, let me just say that I am, in no way, shape or form a financial professional. I'm not a CPA, day-trader or anything like that.

At the time of this writing, I'm a 31 year-old married man, who has been running his own video-production business full-time for a couple of years. My wife and I moved into our first home last year. While we don't have any children (yet), our house is plenty full with 2 cats and 2 dogs. My wife has a full-time job that allows her to work from home and she also has her own marketing/branding business on the side. I say all this to not make you think we have it figured out, because we don't. Something that has been a challenge for us (and chances are for you as well if you're reading this), has been building up our savings/overall wealth and we only have ourselves to blame.

So, what's stopping you from putting this book down? In an attempt to bulk up our savings, I have come up with a few ideas for boosting the available cash we have to put away and I believe these tips and tricks can work for anyone, even those working minimum wage jobs. Even if you made it this far into this short read, let me just say, "thank you." Writing books is outside my wheel-house, so hopefully you not only find these ideas easy to digest, but helpful in your own lives.

Everything you will read has to do with only saving and finding more money you already have to save; there's no need for you to get another job or do something like start an OnlyFans page. There will also be no talk of investing. Every financial advisor will tell you that you need to have adequate savings first before you even think of investing your money and I think that's very sound advice. That topic is potentially for Book #2...

We Suck At Saving

As a society, we're *terrible* at not spending our hard-earned cash. Even before record inflation and unemployment as a result of the COVID-19 pandemic, over half of Americans couldn't cover a $1000 emergency with funds from their savings. Even those with higher incomes live paycheck to paycheck and don't tuck away enough. There are factors outside of our control that unfortunately, impact our incomes. But, there is one thing that *everyone* can do to put aside just even a few more dollars per week.

Stop spending as much money. Thanks for reading, everyone.

Ok, let's dive into that a little more. There are some expenses that are unavoidable: Mortgages, rent, groceries and utilities. But, there are things that we can do to curb our spending in other areas (and even in the above) and have more money to save. Before we do that, we need to talk about *where* to save. That starts with a high-yield savings account.

Where You Save Your Money Matters. A Lot.

When you hear "interest", or "interest rates", you might think about accumulating credit card debt or someone struggling to pay off their car. However, high interest rates can also work in your favor when it comes to saving money in the form of a high-yield savings account, especially with continuing inflation. The bank you have a checking account with might not offer a savings account with a great interest rate and that's ok. There's nothing stopping you from having your main checking account with one bank and a savings account with another.

Speaking from personal experience, I cannot recommend a savings account from Ally Bank enough. The interest rate for our savings account is currently 3.4% and I know there are other banks that offer something similar, or even higher. Just do your homework.

I need to go on record and say that I am not paid by Ally or any other businesses that are mentioned. Again, this is just my personal experience and I mention these companies in the hope that they help lead you in the right direction for your own savings journey. That being said, here's why Ally's awesome.

Besides the interest rate, they have so many ways to help you save more money. The first way, which any savings account from any bank should offer, is the ability to set up recurring transfers. Even if you're on a really tight budget or don't make a lot of money, you can just start a recurring transfer of just $5 or $10 a week. That's something that just about everyone should be able to do. It might not seem like a lot at first, but if you set it and forget it, your savings will begin to build. This is why it's important to choose where to save your money, because a high-interest rate in savings will add even more money into your account through interest payments. I'm pretty sure just about everyone knows that, but it would be silly to not write about increasing your savings without mentioning it.

Back to Ally. Some other features that I have found incredibly helpful are: Surprise Savings, Round-Ups, and the ability to categorize your savings account in Buckets. It's important to note that you need to also have an Ally checking account for these features, so if you happen to be looking for a new bank, here are some good reasons to consider Ally.

With Surprise Savings enabled, Ally analyzes how much money I have in my checking account and automatically calculates a safe amount to transfer over to my savings account every Monday, Wednesday and Friday, transferring no more than $100 at a time. If Ally thinks that I don't have enough money to transfer over, then it won't. Ally has never automatically taken out too much that I have to worry about not being able to cover my regular expenses.

If you have an Acorns account, Ally's round-up system literally works exactly like theirs. For those that don't, here's how it works: Let's say my electricity bill for the month is $48.39. With round-ups enabled, Ally keeps track of the change required to round that transaction up to $49, preemptively setting aside that extra $0.61. Once you hit $5 in "change", Ally transfers that $5 from your checking to your savings account. This applies to every transaction of money out of your checking account, excluding other transfers to your savings account.

This last feature isn't a tool to boost your savings, but it's a powerful way to keep them organized. With Buckets, you can split up your savings account into different categories: emergencies, vacation fund, car payments and more. You can not only set up goals for each bucket to help keep yourself on track, but you can also enable Round-Ups, Surprise Savings, your automatic transfers and even the interest you earn to go into separate buckets automatically.

I hope all of the above hasn't sounded too much like a promo for Ally, but their savings accounts and the tools they offer have been game-changing for me and my wife. If you don't want to go with Ally, I'm sure other banks offer similar tools. But, if nothing else, pay attention to a bank's interest rates, and get a recurring transfer set up from your checking account immediately. Even just $5 a week is a great starting point and when you feel comfortable, start increasing that amount!

This might seem like common sense, but I'm going to say it anyway. *You can not save money if you're spending the money you're trying to save.* If you're on track with your savings and see a number with two or three zeros behind it, you might be tempted to splurge on something. Step away from your computer or put your phone down, then go outside and touch some grass. Building up healthy savings requires discipline. Do not deviate from this course.

This All Sounds Great, But I Can't Afford To Save...

False. Literally anyone can save $5 a week. Anyone. It might require some changes and sacrifice, but do not tell yourself you can't.

We all spend too much money in different areas, myself included. Remember that I'm not a financial professional talking down to you; I'm no better than Plumber Joe and I know there are areas that I can improve in. One reason I'm writing this book is to hold myself accountable and re-evaluate where I can make better financial decisions. One specific category that I'm actively working on – and I'm sure you can as well – is food.

Food is a necessary area for us to spend money in, as we literally need to eat it multiple times a day to survive. But, we can all make better choices on where we spend our money to eat. Look back through your bank and credit card statements for the past month, and see how many times you ate out, whether that's fast-food, restaurants, DoorDash, etc. It's probably more than you realize.

This is the easiest thing we can all do to have more money to save: stop eating out all the gosh darn time. You don't even need to go cold-turkey. If you're eating out two or three times a week, limit yourself to once a week. Then, change that to once every two weeks. Almost all of your regular everyday meals should be created from food you buy from the grocery store. If you're saying to yourself, "I don't know what to buy", "I don't know how to cook" or, "cooking takes too much time and I'm busy", quit being a b*tch. Sorry. But not really.

If you don't know what to buy or how to cook, let me introduce you to this website called Google. Literally millions of recipes for all lifestyles and complexities are online, for free. You'll most likely have to scroll through someone's drawn out, SEO-boosting story of how the chicken parmesan recipe you're trying to find was passed down from somebody's grandma who emigrated from Estonia, but it's there, at the bottom of the webpage.

Planning ahead is also crucial. Figure out what you want to eat for the next week for all the meals you'll eat everyday and *stick to that list*. This is one area that my wife and I are working on being better at. We are both committed to eating the same thing for breakfast and lunch literally everyday (smoothies and lunch meat sandwiches), then having different meals for dinner every night. I'm not going to lie, it's tempting some days to switch it up and get something else for lunch occasionally, but have the mental fortitude to stick to whatever home meal plans you create for yourself. Eventually, it becomes second nature. I used to get tired of having the same meal-replacement vanilla smoothies and sandwiches everyday. Now, it's second nature and my body actually craves those items instead of Sonic or Little Caesars.

Ok, let's get back to groceries. You're committed to finding more money to save, which means you've sat down, figured out your meals for the week you're going to prepare at home, then it's off to Safeway. Before you go running through the aisles picking out all of your ingredients for the week and any staples you need to restock (salt/pepper, butter, etc.), pay attention to the brands you're buying from. For a quick example, let's look at coffee.

I know coffee is what everyone goes to when people talk about cutting back spending, but they do it for good reason. Coffee you buy at Starbucks, for example, is expensive. You might as well go to a Starbucks, take out $10 and set it on fire in the parking lot. If you really, *really* like Starbucks and can't go without it, you might think, "well, Starbucks sells coffee in stores and I'll save money by buying their grounds and be my own barista at home!" That's a good start, but instead of burning $10 in the Starbucks parking lot, you're burning it in your kitchen. This causes your smoke detector to go off and while it's beeping, you're trying to find your broom and/or step ladder to push the very small OFF button that's not easy to find so your dogs stop barking at you. Sorry about that metaphor getting a little carried away, but you catch my drift.

Anyway, coffee. Let's look at what Walmart, for instance, sells different kinds of coffee for. On their website, they are selling 28 ounces of Starbucks' ground coffee for $19.24. 28 ounces sounds like a decent amount of coffee for that price, right? Here's what Walmart is selling their own brand of coffee grounds for: $8.92. That's also for 30 ounces of coffee. You can get more coffee for less than half the cost of Starbucks' brand in the grocery store.

We can also take this a step further and compare Walmart coffee to Walmart coffee and the size of the containers they sell in. Walmart also has their ground coffee available in a 48 ounce container for $10.92. When you're comparing the 48 ounce to the 30 ounce container, based strictly on the listed price, you'd think you'd want to go with the 30 ounce container. While the 48 ounce container has a bigger upfront cost, it's actually less expensive in the long-run, because the price is calculated per ounce. The 48 ounce container is priced at $0.23 per ounce, while the 30 ounce container is priced at $0.29 per ounce. You're paying less for a bigger supply of coffee.

If you're like 98% of Americans and need to drink coffee to start your day and are buying Starbucks, McDonald's or even Folger's, you can save money instantly by buying Walmart's giant container of coffee instead. Instant extra cash generated to put into your savings. You could also take it a step further and stop buying/drinking coffee altogether, but this is a book about saving money, not living a life of misery.

People might also not realize just how many products grocery stores sell under their own brand. I'm not going to list every store and what their respective brands are, but they all have one. If you're worried that there might be a dip in quality from a store brand, there's not. Their sliced cheese is just as good as Kraft's.

Don't forget to also check out coupons or discounts that grocery stores offer. Just make sure that you're not buying products *just because* they're on sale. Instead, keep track of these offers and take advantage when an item you need is available at a discounted price. It also doesn't cost as much as you think it does to eat healthy. Foods and meals that are high in protein and fiber especially will keep you feeling full longer, which means less food you have the urge to eat and therefore, buy. It's also important to note that if you do find a coupon for something like Starbucks' fancy ground coffee, still cross-check with the other brands that are available. Even with the discounted price, those Starbucks coffee grounds still might not be the most cost-effective option.

One more note. Earlier in this chapter, when I said to stick to your shopping list, I meant it. Stay committed to buying what's only written down on your shopping list that you created at home before getting to the store. Don't grab an extra bag of chips or a microwavable burrito (and don't ask me how many times I've done that). It's also a good idea to go grocery shopping after you've had a meal; you're more likely to stick to your list if you're not shopping on an empty stomach.

One final note. Plan a couple of different meals around the same main ingredient (chicken, beef, pasta) and buy those items in the larger packaging. This seems like a very doable plan for cutting food costs, right? Great. Let's talk about cell phones.

Verizon Is Ripping You Off

Not just Verizon, but also AT&T, T-Mobile and Sprint. No matter how many commercials with Kate McKinnon or Matthew Stafford you see, don't buy what they're selling. I'll talk about my experience.

For over a year, I had a Verizon, unlimited 5G Data Plan that cost me $87/month. They weren't even giving me 5G coverage where I lived! Sure, I probably didn't need the unlimited data, but even if I had one of their other plans, I'd still be paying too much.

A few months ago, I switched to Mint Mobile. It was around Thanksgiving when I made this switch, so I just happened to catch a Black Friday special they were offering, which was buy three months and get three months free. Out of the gate, I paid just $72 for six months of coverage; I was ecstatic about that. But, what about after those six months were up? I went ahead and changed my plan to auto-renew in twelve month increments, with Mint's twelve month plans costing just $240 for 10GB of data per month. Remember, this was for coverage *after* the 6 months I already paid for had passed. Effectively, for eighteen total months of cell coverage, I paid $312. $312 would have gotten me a little over 3 months of coverage on my Verizon plan. Oh, I also have awesome 5G coverage at my house now.

Verizon was nice enough to include an Apple Music subscription in my plan, so I lost that when I switched. However, even with the cost of an Apple Music subscription I pay for myself now ($11/month), I'm still saving hundreds of dollars a year.

There are plenty of other good options out there besides Mint. Do a little bit of research to find a plan/carrier that fits your needs and you can have that much more money to put in your savings account in just a couple of weeks.

A Social Life Comes With A Price Tag

No, you don't need to be an isolated hermit that never hangs out with your friends to save money. But, if you're going out every weekend (or multiple nights in a week), I don't think I want to look at your account balances.

My wife and I are big fans of microbreweries and there are dozens where we live. Beer doesn't cost as much as a margarita, but the amount that you can spend does sneak up on you. It certainly did for us. Just like with eating out, if you think you're going out to bars or breweries too much, just scale it back slowly but surely. Going out – especially if alcohol is involved – also means making sure you have a way to get home safely. If you're not driving your own car to and from places, which you need to spend money on gas to drive, Uber is just another expense that can get out of hand quickly. Speaking from personal experience, a night on the town with alcohol involved also means Taco Bell gets invited to the party. More money that disappears before your eyes.

You can still have fun, of course; life is meant to be enjoyed. Just don't do it every weekend. Your wallet and liver will thank you.

Being Thrifty Is Nifty

How often do you buy clothes, shoes and other accessories? Where do you shop? If your closet or shoe rack is at capacity, this is an area where you can easily save.

You also don't need to buy clothes first-hand. There is nothing wrong with getting apparel from places like Goodwill or Salvation Army; they don't sell anything that isn't good quality and people from all tax brackets take advantage of these stores. Sure, you might be at the mercy of what donations they have or haven't received, but I have yet to be inside a place that isn't well-stocked. There's also plenty of thrift stores in any decent-sized populated area, if there's something you can't find at one store. If you drive around town to different boutique stores anyway, what's the difference?

Bonus tip for some extra money: Sell clothes you have and don't want to wear anymore on eBay. My wife does this regularly and consistently makes sales. If you also sell something on eBay you bought at the Salvation Army you want to part ways with, you can even make a little profit.

Streaming Services Wash Your Money Away

It's Saturday night and you're saving some money by staying in. Your feet are propped up in some cozy slippers you copped from a second-hand store and are about to rip open a bag of Kroger's pretzels. With your new, cheaper cell phone plan, you text a couple of friends to invite them over. Once they show up, you guys decide to put something on the TV, but don't know what. You scroll through Netflix, Hulu, Disney+, HBO Max, Showtime, Peacock, Mega Hallmark Christmas, Paramo—

Wait, how many streaming services are you paying for again?

In the infancy of streaming TV shows and movies, the main allure of these services was that they cost less than cable or satellite TV. If you bought one or two subscriptions, that was accurate. These days, however, there are more streaming services than Nick Cannon has kids. It's very, very easy to set up a subscription to all of these services and forget you're paying for them. Is that beeping your smoke detector going off again?

You don't need to go crazy and stop paying for all of them. If you are paying for a handful of streaming services, just take an honest look and think about how much you actually use them. Just canceling one service is instant cash to save. While you're at it, review your statements to make sure there aren't any other subscriptions you're paying for that you don't use. There's also nothing wrong with making a concerted effort to start using them again, if you think they're worth holding onto and paying for. Subscriptions are only a waste of money if you don't use them and they don't spark joy.

Giving Credit Cards Credit Where It's Due

Here's one last area where I think, if handled responsibly, can help so many people find extra cash to save. If you don't have a credit card, don't be scared of getting one! Everything negative you hear about them stems from people being dumb with how they use theirs. Where we get into serious trouble is when we put more charges on our credit cards than we can afford and helplessly watch interest accumulate.

Don't be dumb with credit cards. Only use them to pay what you know, with 1000% confidence, you can afford every month. Also, avoid credit cards that come with annual fees. Those are very silly and unnecessary.

Ok, so what kind of credit card should I get and how can getting one help me find extra money to save? Credit cards that offer cash back rewards are your golden ticket. I have two that I use (and yes, pay off in full every month) that have been awesome.

The first one I have and the one I've had the longest is Capital One's Quicksilver card. Every purchase I make with this card qualifies for a 1.5% cash back reward. 1.5% isn't a lot, but it adds up. You can do a lot of things with this cash back balance once you let it accrue, but I only use it to lower my credit card balance by reimbursing myself for purchases I made with the card. Let those rewards sit for long enough without touching them and you can eventually cover an entire billing cycle! All you have to do is use the card within your financial means and pay it off in full every month. Easy money.

As nice as my Capital One credit card is, the other one I make use of is even better: the Amazon Prime Rewards credit card. Yes, you do need to have a Prime membership to be eligible for this card, so if you can't afford a membership, there are plenty of other excellent credit cards out there. But, if you find some extra money from cutting back on other expenses to afford a Prime membership, it is absolutely worth it anyway.

With the Prime Rewards credit card, you get 1% back on every transaction. Not as good as my Quicksilver card, sure. But, if you use it at restaurants or gas stations, you get 2% cash back. Nice. Where the fun really begins, though, is with purchases you make on Amazon... 5% cash back. Holy guacamole. And yes, you can use this Prime Rewards credit card to pay for your Prime membership. I did the math and that's an extra $9.95 in your pocket every year from just one transaction.

The Prime credit card reflects your rewards in the form of Amazon "points". You can use these points in a number of different ways, but the two I have grown fond of are using those points to pay for items I buy on Amazon and lowering my monthly credit card balance. This book is about saving money, so I'm not advocating for you to go on an insane online shopping spree just to accrue points with this card. Fortunately, there are thousands of necessary household items that you can buy on Amazon and pay for with this card. You can also take your savings a step further with these items you need to buy and set up Subscribe and Save.

If there's one item that literally everyone needs to have in their house, it's toilet paper. You can buy toilet paper on Amazon and have it shipped to your home regularly through Subscribe and Save. Just by setting up having toilet paper dropped off at your front door through Amazon, you save 5% on it. That 5% is different from the 5% cash back you get from the Prime Rewards credit card, by the way; it's literally a 5% discount on toilet paper. In case you were wondering, Amazon also has their own brand of toilet paper, which means cheaper toilet paper you can buy.

Why stop there? Set up Subscribe and Save for paper towels, sponges, dish soap, laundry detergent, dog food. If you have enough products that you need to buy anyway, the 5% savings jump up to 15% when you have five or more items in the same auto delivery! Pay for these products with your Prime Rewards card and you still get the 5% cash back on top of those savings. Use your accrued Amazon points to lower your credit card balance every month and you'll start to sit on a small pile of Benjamins.

Last year, I accumulated over $200 in Amazon points, which I used to either cover purchases I made on Amazon or lower my monthly credit card balance. This year, my wife and I are going all-in on Subscribe and Save, which means I'll have even more points at my disposal to lower my credit card balances even further. The best part about Subscribe and Save is this: You don't need a Prime membership to use it and it's 100% free. So, you have the convenience of these essential household items delivered to your house without ever worrying about running out; you can also have item deliveries skipped or shipped ahead of schedule if you need; you also potentially save money on gas by not having to make emergency runs for toilet paper. I don't mean to be talking about toilet paper again, but we originally set up Subscribe and Save for toilet paper right when COVID hysteria was at its peak. I don't think my wife and I will ever make a decision that smart again.

I want to reiterate this one point, because it's so important: with the great power of cashback credit cards comes great responsibility. You have to pay these credit cards off in full every month or else you risk losing these rewards. All that extra money you dreamed of having to save can be wiped out instantly by interest. Be smart and your savings account will be in excellent shape. Quicksilver and Prime Rewards also aren't the only credit cards out there that offer great cashback rewards. Go on a site like NerdWallet, which has already done the heavy lifting and compare some really great options.

Saving The Best For Last

I know that there's plenty of other ways to save money besides the ones I discussed. Some take longer than others, so I just wanted to share a couple of ideas that I know personally can have an instant impact. Hopefully, you saw that anyone can save just a few extra dollars with a couple of simple decisions and planning.

Another way to make sure you are saving is to set goals for yourself. The first thing that anyone should save up for is to be ready for any emergency. What would you do if your car breaks down? Or if your dog eats a sock and needs to go to the Vet's emergency room (or if it happens more than once, like with my wife's and my dog)?

Money set aside for any and all emergencies is vital. A good rule of thumb any financial planner will tell you is to have enough saved up to cover 3-6 months of your regular expenses. It might take some people longer to get there than others, but literally anyone can do that if they make the right financial decisions and have patience.

Once you hit your emergency savings goal, why stop there? Create a vacation fund. If you're living in an apartment and have dreams of owning a home, get to work on saving up for your down payment. If you want to start your own business or become self-employed through freelance work, you can do what with confidence knowing you can still pay your rent on-time as you get started. And as great as a high-interest savings account is, you can make that extra cash you've gotten into the habit of setting aside work even harder for you by investing. If you're new to investing, it might seem overwhelming, but you can just start with an app or software like Acorns. Knowing that you can have a metaphorical cushion full of soft cash opens your world up to endless possibilities to increase your personal wealth. Like I said at the beginning, I'm no expert in the world of finances, but I'm committed to making the right changes in my life and hopefully you now are as well.

www.ingramcontent.com/pod-product-compliance
Lightning Source LLC
Chambersburg PA
CBHW071147220526
45467CB00015B/2107